Codi {Codes} and the Carrot Cake

To Ester and Leo

Written By
Sergi Fornés

Illustrated by
Daniel Limon

One morning, **Codi** and her friends, **Katie**, **Joe** and robot **Beep**, asked Codi's mom for one of their favourite cakes:

"Hi Mom, could you make us one of your delicious **carrot cakes**?"

"I would," sighed Codi's mom. "But this is everything we have left from the carrots in our garden. A **rabbit** has eaten them all! I need to catch it before I plant more carrots."

Katie's eyes lit up. "We can help you with that, Mrs. Codes!" she said.

"OK, it's **Algotime!**"

Codi started to plan. "We will need a trap." she said. "We will put some food inside, and when the rabbit enters, we will pull the rope and the trap will close."

"But the rabbit will see us," Katie worried.

"I have an idea," Joe cried. "Beep and I will hide close to the trap. Codi and you will watch from further away. When you see the rabbit inside the box, you will let us know and we will pull the rope."

"So, this is the algorithm:"

Codi and Katie:

when rabbit enters trap

broadcast pull

Joe & Beep:

when I receive pull

pull rope

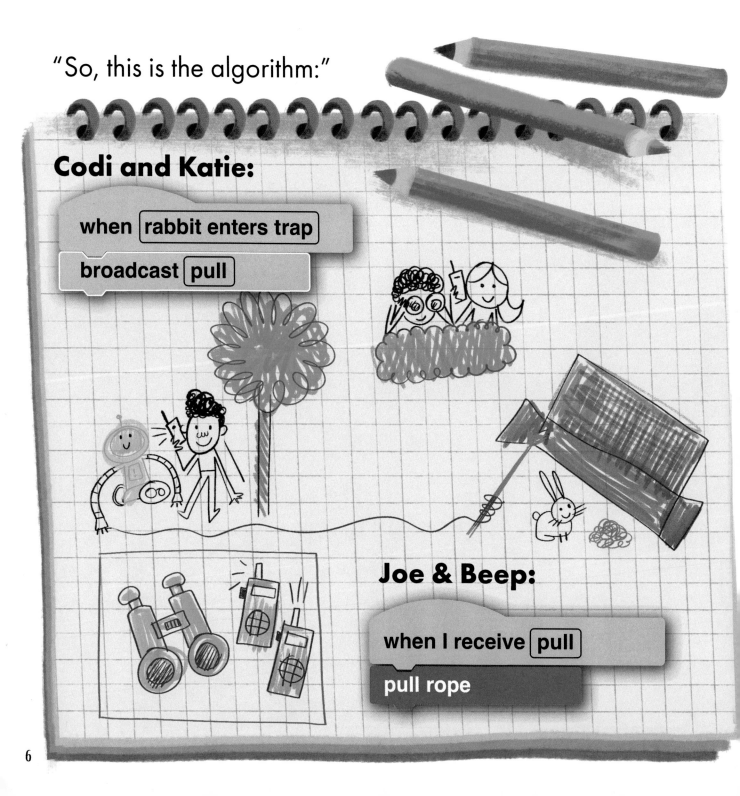

"**Let's do it!**," they all agreed.

The kids are ready.

Beep pulled the rope... but nothing happened, and the rabbit hopped away.

Katie run over. "We were making the signal. Why didn't you pull the rope?" she asked.

"We did, but the rabbit is smarter than what we thought. **It has bitten the rope!**" Joe cried.

"We need a **new plan**," Codi said thoughtfully. Suddenly, Katie jumped up, "I have a plan! I'll catch you, rabbit!"

Then she sat back down with a sigh. "Actually I don't think that would work... never mind."

"Let's think about this," Joe turned to his friends. "Our rope is broken. We will have to be very close to activate the trap. Only if we could get close without being seen...", Joe explained.

"I know, **Beep can do it!**", Codi said.

"We will camouflage Beep to look like a plant. Then Beep can slowly move closer, and when the rabbit gets inside the trap, Beep will activate it.

It's **Algotime**:"

Beep, beep?

Beep:

repeat until `can reach the trap`
    if `rabbit can see you` then
        stand still
    else
        move **1** steps

wait until `rabbit is inside`
activate trap

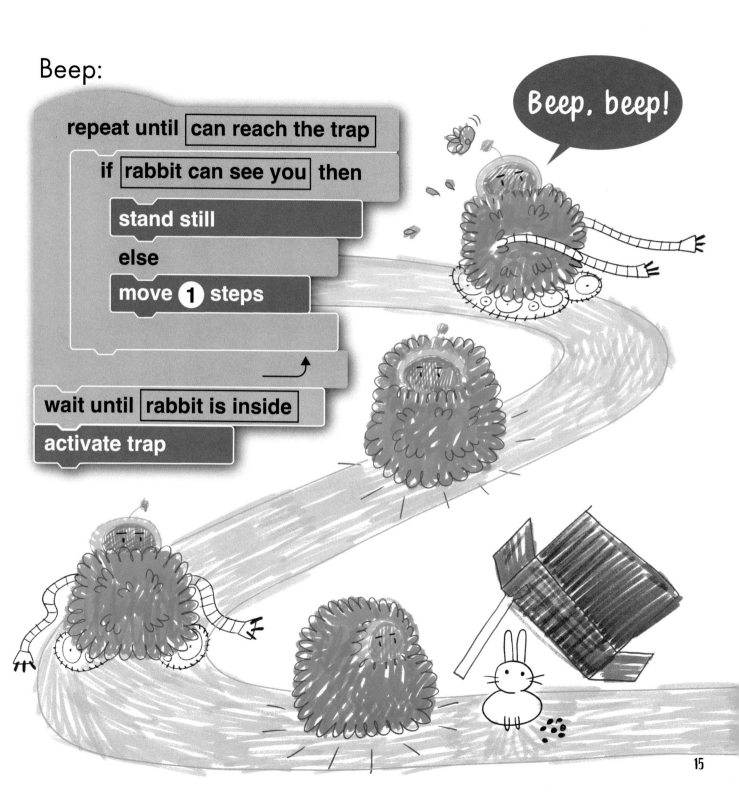

The kids caught the rabbit! They carefully lifted the trap and carried the rabbit to a safe place in the forest.

"Here, we are far enough away from the garden now," Joe said.

Beep opened the trap and let the rabbit free. "Off you go buddy. Do not come back to our garden to eat Mom's carrots again, please!", Codi called.

21

"Mom, we have taken care of the rabbit," Codi said.

"It is far away from your vegetable garden now, Mrs. Codes!" Katie nodded.

"That's wonderful news! Thank you, all!" smiled Codi's mum. "Now who's hungry? I have made your second favourite: raspberry cake!"

23

Baking a Carrot Cake

Let's learn how to bake Codi's favourite carrot cake with an algorithm!

Ingredients

For the cake:

- 350g self-raising flour
- 325g sugar
- 2 tsp cinnamon
- 250g grated carrots
- 75g chopped walnuts
- 4 eggs
- 200ml oil
- 4 tbsp milk
- For the icing:
- 180g cream cheese
- 30g icing sugar

You will also need:

- 22cm round cake tin

Instructions

preheat the oven (180°c)

add | cake ingredients | to a bowl

mix

pour mix into a cake tin

put tin in the oven

wait **30** min

remove from oven

wait until | cold |

add | icing ingredients | to a bowl

mix

decorate top with icing

24

Made in the USA
Las Vegas, NV
18 December 2024